SUMMARY
& ANALYSIS

OF

THE MOMENT
OF LIFT

*How Empowering Women
Changes the World*

A GUIDE TO THE BOOK
BY MELINDA GATES

NOTE: This book is a summary and analysis and is meant as a companion to, not a replacement for, the original book.
Please follow this link to purchase a copy of the original book: https://amzn.to/2Jabgri

TABLE OF CONTENTS

SYNOPSIS

The Moment of Lift is the story of how change is sparked when women are empowered, and lives are counted equally. There are nine chapters, each exploring themes which have formed the basis of the work at the Bill and Melinda Gates Foundation. It includes eye-opening statistics, lessons, and discoveries that have impacted Melinda Gates since her philanthropic work began over two decades ago.

Melinda describes the journey from setting up the foundation to combat extreme poverty to wielding it as a catalyst for the empowerment of women. Tucked between the stories of heroes and changemakers are snippets from her childhood, her early Microsoft career, her family life with Bill and their three children, and her evolution as a feminist.

The first four chapters cover maternal and newborn health, family planning, and girls' education. Chapter five, halfway, is a fitting display of values central to Melinda's philosophy in life. It also reveals her most private, defining moments.

Chapters six through eight describe the dangers of inequality with unpaid work, child marriage, women in agriculture and the workplace, and the role of equal partnership in a better world. Chapter nine closes her story with a call to action, citing an example of how their program helped sex workers in India find their voices and stand together.

CHAPTER 1: THE LIFT OF A GREAT IDEA

Melinda introduces herself, not as the wife of Bill Gates, but as a woman, mother, Microsoft tech, and feminist. She tells of the journey which brought her to that point of confidence and the beginnings of the foundation which changed her life.

Key Takeaway: The Bill and Melinda Gates Foundation was a side project at first.

Passionate about giving everyone access to the growing technology field, they started small. Companies like Microsoft had the power to bring software to people on the ground and Melinda and Bill first started by donating computers to public libraries. They knew more projects like these were needed and they invited the enthusiastic Patty Stonesifer (a Microsoft retiree) to run the nationwide effort volunteering her time 'in a tiny office above a pizza parlor.'

Melinda herself was heavily influenced by the technology introduced to her girls' high school by a teacher (who had pressed the issue with the principal, done classes at a local university to learn how to teach computers, and singlehandedly inspired Melinda to pursue it as a career).

Key Takeaway: The Gates family grew at the rate they desired, and Melinda was a stay-at-home mother.

As her travels took her around the world, Melinda would increasingly realize how much her own life had been shaped by equality (and inequality) between men and women. Her choice was to stay home as a mother, to have three children, three years apart, after ten years at a successful career. It was timed thanks to birth control and the ability to conceive as and when she was ready.

This privilege was something she took for granted. After many years of doing work among the poorest women of the world, she could not deny the incessant need for family planning options across nations. These women, who were not as fortunate, all told her the same story: the choice to plan their families on their own terms would save lives.

Key Takeaway: Melinda played in the big leagues but avoided the stage for as long as possible.

A shy person by nature who coveted her privacy, especially in her family life (being the wife of the world-famous Bill Gates), Melinda fought hard to stay out of the limelight. She knew important and influential people from all over the globe and used these contacts to exact meaningful change including the development and distribution of vaccines in developing countries. She was intricately involved in each aspect of The Foundation's work but could not justify stepping into the public eye.

That changed when she realized the magnitude of the family planning problem in the poorest regions of the world. By then she had spoken to thousands of women worldwide, witnessed their daily struggles, and heard their pleas for contraceptives on their own terms. She had also seen countless reports on how a lack of family planning is the root of so many other problems, including the leading cause of death in teenage girls.

As a Catholic, she understood the implications of speaking up on the political and religious bombshell, but by 2012 she had made up her mind. She agreed to cosponsor a summit in the United Kingdom on family planning.

Contraceptives were pledged for 120 million more women by the end of 2019 in an inspiring campaign titled FP 2020. Tanzania, Rwanda, Uganda, Kenya, Burkina Faso, and Senegal were key in raising both funds and awareness. And the UK doubled their efforts, too.

It was a roaring success, but now her fellow advocates wanted more from her. She wasn't ready for more, still reeling from the genital-cutting interviews she had done in Senegal before the summit. She quit twice in one week but eventually accepted she had to continue in the work, however heartbreaking it may have been.

Key Takeaway: Their great idea was lifting women up.

As the foundation took her to all corners of the globe, Melinda's discovery was like an 'awakening' that continued to spread and take wing. She realized the numbers spoke to the truth she saw in the poorest (and richest) places on earth: poverty thrived where women were limited, and prosperity reigned where they were empowered.

From that moment, she decided to be more intentional about investing in women, knowing that this spark worldwide transformation—as the single most powerful catalyst for the upliftment of the poor and oppressed.

CHAPTER 2: EMPOWERING MOTHERS

The chapter discusses the development of the philanthropic work that Melinda started. The official foundation platform was as a way for Bill and Melinda to give back from their abundant wealth, but also to see a difference in the world around them.

They were appalled at the deaths of children in the poorest of nations, purely a result of their abject poverty. Children are dying because of their mothers' collective inability to care for them, lacking nutrition, vaccines, education, and caring adults while both parents are at work. The problem was multifaceted, but to help poor mothers protect their own children through the alleviation of extreme poverty seemed the best solution.

Melinda speaks of her contact with people like Hans Rosling, the famous Swedish physician who died in 2017. The man made an enormous impact on her, sharing his hard-learned lessons.

She tells stories of successful interventions for mothers and newborns by Agnes, the amazing health minister in post-war Rwanda, Ati, a young birth attendant from Indonesia, and Vishwajeet and Aarti who have done remarkable work in the poorest places in India.

Key Takeaway: Delivery systems are almost more important than the aid dispatched.

One of the lessons Melinda learned early on is that aid was not enough. The delivery system was crucial to penetrating age-old traditional practices and human behavior.

She witnessed a phenomenal program in one of the poorest states in India, Uttar Pradesh. There, Saksham, an organization that focused on maternal and newborn care, was working miracles in the place where ten percent of the world's newborn deaths occur annually.

The Saksham team weren't using technology, either. They were promoting training and skills development for carers, midwives, and support figures for during and after birth.

The message was basic, including:

- Promoting skin-to-skin to keep the baby warm and help develop immunity

- Breastfeeding from birth instead of waiting three days as the religious leaders advised

- Other hygiene practices that defied traditional convention in the villages, like not giving the infant water (because of the high contamination risk in the area)

The results were astonishing. Saksham's work helped reduce newborn deaths by half in just a eighteen months! Melinda remains adamant that the delivery system should shape the strategy of aid work, and that fighting poverty starts with empowering women.

Key Takeaway: Barriers are formed when people are excluded.

Melinda passionately reveals the cause of so much suffering for the people on the 'margins' of society. She reminds us that we push people away when we recognize something in them that we don't want to acknowledge in ourselves.

"This is the core remedy for poverty and almost any social ill— including the excluded, going to the margins of society and bringing everybody back in" (Gates, p. 50).

We don't want to get old, sick, or poor, so we push away these groups of people and justify to ourselves that we are better than them, more deserving of the privileged positions in which we find ourselves. Her mantra resonates that everyone deserves access to healthcare, wealth, choices, and life abundance—because we are all human beings and equality is right.

CHAPTER 3: FAMILY PLANNING

As Melinda's focus on newborn and maternal health expanded, she began to realize that this was not the primary issue. These women didn't want help birthing children. Their plea was a desperate cry for the choice of when (and if) to fall pregnant in the first place.

The chapter is an extended analysis of the historical dialogue around family planning (still rutted in stigma and misogyny). Even in the United States, contraceptives were not made freely available to unmarried women until 1972. In countries suffering from the highest levels of poverty today, there is a direct correlation with the availability and acceptance of contraceptives.

Key Takeaway: Contraceptives are key to fighting extreme poverty and protecting women's health.

A new development in the history of the world, contraceptives have only been 'legalized' (even by developed countries) in the last few decades. Before, a woman was seen in the light of her role as a child bearer, which could not be separated from her individuality, her ambitions, and her decisions apart from a man.

It's a conversation that was started in earnest thanks to women like Margaret Sanger, who championed contraceptives in 1916 despite consecutive arrests, public humiliation, and conviction for her activities. She was fighting against the Anthony Comstock worldview for recognition that a woman is a person in her own right, too.

Melinda and others are now trying to change the global conversation on family planning to one of basic women's rights and empowerment. The dialogue has long been entrenched in nauseating political issues like eugenics, abortion, and sterilization in the name of 'population control' which became popular in the 1960s. It has been a challenge beyond expectation and much still needs to be done to change the public perception of contraceptives for women.

Melinda believes this single issue has the power to heal the world of extreme poverty—especially in countries where women are still forced into marriages as young teenagers, and where childbearing is linked to superstitions and cultural stigmas and status.

Key Takeaway: Melinda's role in the global conversation was criticized heavily by the Catholic church.

Informed by her faith and the teachings of the church, Melinda felt the call to humanitarian work as a natural extension of the Biblical command to 'love thy neighbor.' After her successful family planning summit in 2012, however, the criticism launched against her in the media was grievous.

She expected it, of course, as a practicing, professing Catholic, but it still came as a shock. It forced her into clear introspection of her motives and convictions. Her conclusion was that she was acting in love, and that this was more important than the manmade laws of the Catholic church.

Answering the plea of a woman to live longer and care for their existing children was love, which could not be denied no matter the doctrine behind the contradiction.

Key Takeaway: Softening a culture steeped in stigma takes time.

By 2016, Kenya was way ahead in their goals from the 2012 conference and Melinda wanted to find out why. Her discovery was that the data wasn't inclusive of the whole story behind why women were or weren't using contraceptives in an area.

Questionnaires neglected to capture the husband who turned away contraceptives being offered on door-to-door visits, the woman who was being told by her church that she had no choice, the teenage mother who barely escaped domestic violence and could not make enough to feed her existing children, never mind afford a trip to the clinic or contraceptives. The data was incomplete, and the conversation was still new to slow-changing cultural norms.

Male advocates for the conversation were badly needed, too. The United States, a leader in global family planning policies, is also on the brink of reversing its progress with proposed funding cuts that will affect one-and-a-half million women in-country. It's another example of laws for women being made by men and hopefully, the result of the backlash will be even more passion for the rights of women overall.

CHAPTER 4: GIRLS IN SCHOOLS

It's another 'old story' in the modern world of women's rights activism, but education for girls is still a pressing issue on the global stage. When girls are given an education equal to that of their male counterparts, everyone wins.

Key Takeaway: Girls need education; girls want education.

As the conversation on family planning evolved, Melinda discovered that it wasn't enough to pull people out of extreme poverty. They needed more. Specifically, they needed to get their girls into schools and start a cycle of positive transformation that would last for generations to come.

Good schools, too, are places which inspire, empower, and change students into people who recognize their own strengths and capabilities.

Key Takeaway: Educating girls is still controversial in many parts of the world.

The statistics are clear: girls are being educated less than boys, even in 2019. This has been especially visible in secondary education (which then extends into tertiary education). The problem is a cultural one, reinforced by the traditional view of (male) lawmakers that 'the role of the woman is to serve the man.'

Malala Yousafzai is but one extreme example of how entrenched this view is in many parts of the world. The fifteen-year-old girl was shot by the Taliban for her activism in Pakistan, and later received the Nobel Peace Prize for her refusal to remain silent despite her escape from a terrible death. She is an example of someone Melinda feels can change the world, empowering local activists to continue the work, and uniting people, but remaining humble.

Key Takeaway: Melinda introduces the Bangladesh Rural Advancement Committee (BRAC).

In Mexico, they started a program called 'Opportunities,' which paid girls a monthly salary equivalent to them going into the workplace to encourage them to come to school. It worked so well that educational parity has now been achieved, and Mexico has the highest percentage of women graduating from computer science programs at a university level. Fifty-two other countries have followed suit with the idea.

The BRAC schools (started by Fazle Hasan Abed), too, are making waves, with forty-eight thousand schools and learning centers around the world. Each BRAC center requires seventy percent female students, all-female teachers (from the same community), and free resources so that costs pose no excuse. Extremists have targeted these BRAC schools by burning them down, but Abed keeps going, rebuilding the schools, because the idea is clearly working for social change.

Key Takeaway: Love is key to lifting people up.

People like Sister Sudha Varghese (who worked with the "rat-eaters" untouchables—the lowest of the low in India), Kakenya Ntaiya (a Kenyan girl who has championed girls education among the Maasai and around the world), and Sona (a ten-year-old whose courage helped lift an entire village out of extreme poverty) are heroes of change.

Ignored by policy discussions and taboo in politically correct debates and aid work, love is the key to supporting people. Love gives power for lasting change and a sense of self-worth. Education is first and foremost in changing one's view of oneself, and this can only happen when you are supported by others and shown that you are worthy of their love and respect.

CHAPTER 5: UNPAID WORK

The unpaid work of housewives (and other informal positions) is discussed as viable for consideration in productivity studies. Melinda also shares how she has tried to raise her children to see the world's citizens as equals, all trying to be happy in their own pursuits.

Key Takeaway: Marilyn Waring pioneered research into women's unpaid work.

A New Zealand economist, her research started in 1975 and has revealed staggering statistics in the field. Never had the work done by millions of homemakers around the world been considered for economic analysis because of the 'free' nature of the work. It was always considered an inevitable part of life, not an opportunity cost keeping people trapped in extreme poverty.

Waring recorded women's unpaid work as being the biggest sector in the global economy and was astounded that economists still refused to count it in official data on work.

Key Takeaway: The theme underlying unpaid work is equal partnership.

Melinda shares candidly about her relationship with Bill in light of creating an equal partnership in their marriage. She believes this is the key to a transformed society and the search for true happiness in life. She also admits that it was the most difficult chapter to write because it opened her up to criticism, vulnerability in a world of hurt.

Her passion for equality (in partnerships, especially in the primary relationship of our lives), stems from a realization that her philanthropic work needed to begin with a transformation of herself. It needed her to have integrity, like an equal partnership in her own marriage before she could help women assert themselves in their own relationships. She and Bill worked hard to share their loads, cultivating respect and love into their daily interactions through hard work and many tears.

Part of this revelation is the admiration she has for her husband, Bill. She praises him for his tenderness and humility, untainted by his enormous achievements and vast wealth. He considers himself 'lucky,' not better than others, a product of his favorable circumstances.

Melinda considers herself a feminist, fighting against male dominance in the world, not because she believes that power should be in the hands of women instead of men. She believes that there should be *no dominance* at all, that we should empower each other as equals, no matter the gender. Equal partnership, and the belief that all lives matter, is the key to breaking this cycle of silent inequality so prevalent across the globe.

CHAPTER 6: CHILD MARRIAGE

Child marriage is still surprisingly prevalent in developing economies. The consequences to the girls are inconceivable. People like Mabel van Oranje are advocating against this issue, but much more needs to be done to discourage the fourteen million child marriages still occurring annually.

Key Takeaway: Child brides suffer intensely.

The girls married off are subject to higher rates of HIV, more abuse, rape, beatings, female genital cutting, little to no educational opportunities, and domination by husbands much older than themselves. They have no chance for respect or equal partnership in their relationships and are often treated as slaves.

Their lives, too, are at risk. Early childbirth is often fatal as the leading cause of death in girls aged 15 to 19 globally. If the child bride doesn't die, her infant may, or the young mother is left with lasting physical trauma (like fistula) and subjected to a degrading life of continuous illness and conditions akin to slavery and poverty.

Key Takeaway: The culture of child marriage is complicated.

When advocates highlight this practice on humanitarian platforms, people are quick to condemn the responsible adults involved. The issue is deeper than simply a black-market euphemism for girl child slavery, however. For the parents of the young girl in a dangerous community, it is often the best option among a handful of bad ones, and they do it from a place of love and desperation.

Child marriage becomes a way for poor families to protect their daughters from abuse sure to come from the men in their neighborhood and their families. It is a way to make life a little better for the rest of their children, too, with money earned from a dowry (or saved from paying a lower dowry for a younger, less educated girl). In their eyes, they are marrying off the girl to save her from rape, sexual abuse, and scarier situations she may encounter through the gender violence rife in her community.

To change the culture of child marriage, one needs to change the culture of gender-based violence so prevalent even in the developed world.

Key Takeaway: Molly Melching, the founder of Tostan, is a pivotal example of how empathy sparks change.

The organization is based in Senegal and has worked tirelessly to end child marriage in the region. Molly started by getting involved in the communities by facilitating conversation, not distributing aid. They talked about all sorts of issues, getting the community members to debate and decide on the type of life they hoped to have in a perfect future.

All the work thereafter was designed to help the community achieve this self-imagined eutopia by opening a dialogue about tradition and life. They offered education on the community's terms, encouraged respectful exchanges during the three weekly discussions, and provided resources to help implement these changes.

The remarkable result? A changed culture from the inside out. Better marriages, better health, more equal partnerships—and no more child marriage in over 8,500 communities in the region.

CHAPTER 7: WOMEN IN AGRICULTURE

By 2006, the foundation had recognized the immense value in agricultural production to combat poverty. They had put effort and resources into developing new seeds and training farmers without making any connections to the gender roles in this regard. Agriculture seemed to be a male-dominated issue, yet when they looked at the fields, there were only women working there.

Key Takeaway: Women farm.

In Sub-Saharan Africa and Southeast Asia (where the foundation's focus lay), women were a prominent feature on the agricultural stage. They farmed the land on top of their other duties, yet received a third less yield than their male counterparts.

The foundation started to focus on empowering women to farm better. They estimated that, if successful, this simple shift in focus would reduce the number of undernourished people in the world by one hundred million at a minimum. It was a phenomenal learning curve and one that impacted (and continues to impact) millions of people on the foundation's receiving end.

Key Takeaway: Women farm equally as well as men but have more barriers to success.

It became clear that women had the same skills as men, but that they were sorely lacking in other crucial resources and the social freedom to enact successful ventures. They didn't have as much land and spent a fraction of the time men did there because of their myriad of household duties. Consequently, women had worse yields, and because they couldn't afford better seeds and fertilizers the next year, experienced poor yields continuously, perpetuating the cycle.

If women were given the credit lines, supplies, marketing opportunities, and free land ownership of men, their farming success would substantially improve. The result would not only be an improvement in the lives of poor women but would extend to the family units and the economies in which they resided. It would not be a ripple effect, but a tsunami of meaningful change for millions of people to escape extreme poverty.

Key Takeaway: The source of discrimination against women is largely male-dominated religions.

The foundation only voiced their 'gender' agenda late in the game, once it had become abundantly clear that empowering women would solve so many of the problems it was addressing in its projects. Once they did, though, things changed rapidly—both in-house and in the public arena.

The chapter ends with a punchy declaration as to the source of the gender-bias problem. The male-dominated religions of history have been prominent in shaping culture and law. Religious men have long used scriptural interpretation to hold up their power.

This skewed (false) interpretation of the faithful is yet another example of men making decisions for women without their input. For meaningful change to happen in every country, the United States included, this wheel needs to be broken.

CHAPTER 8: WOMEN IN THE WORKPLACE

Melinda shares her thoughts on changing a workplace culture to reflect equality and respect owed to all human beings. She tells of her own experiences at Microsoft in her twenties, reflecting on the remarkable people who have shaped her over the years. She also describes the subtle shifts in culture when a false image is shed for the true self beneath.

Key Takeaway: Microsoft was male-dominated and had an aggressive culture.

Used to working in tech as a lone female, Melinda found Microsoft as she had come to expect in the industry: dominated by males who were abrasive and direct, never said thank you, and came down hard on failures or mistakes. She found herself wanting to leave early on but then decided that the excitement of what the company offered was too precious to give up.

Instead, she found ways to be herself and to shed the false mask she was wearing to 'fit in' with the culture. She found allies and colleagues who supported her in this focus and became lifelong friends.

Key Takeaway: Melinda comments on the #MeToo movement.

Following the journey of Susan Fowler (of Uber), and the #MeToo 'silence breakers' who poured in afterward,

Melinda celebrated the empowerment of women, especially in the tech industry. Sharing about her own former unhealthy relationship, she emphasized it wasn't enough until the movement spoke for women without a voice— those without access to social media or support systems or recognition.

The key to equality is diversity, in the workplace and everywhere. She is exceedingly concerned about the infancy of AI being too homogenous in nature, thanks to the non-diverse programmers involved. If AI is going to run the world, we need it to represent the breadth and width of humanity equally, otherwise, existing gender and racial bias will shape the new technological age exactly as it did the centuries before it.

Her point extended to the foundation, too, where changing the culture started with her own willingness to shed her perfectionist exterior. She urged women to take each opportunity to bring equality and empowerment of the gender in the workplace, including advocating for family leave in the workplace and hiring diversely. It's the only way to spark true and lasting change.

CHAPTER 9: THE LIFT OF COMING TOGETHER

Melinda tells the beautiful story of how sex workers in India unified to save their country from a burgeoning HIV epidemic that saved generations of people. They came together, arms linked, voices resounding against those that were seeking to keep them on the fringes of society.

Key Takeaway: The answer to dominance is acceptance and inclusion.

As a parting reminder, we see that dominance is rooted in fear of being marginalized—a proactive measure to exclude those who make us feel vulnerable. Only inclusion will end this power struggle, not another war. Only inclusion has the power to bring people in as equal contributors, valued and loved for the part in it they represent.

Her call is for the acceptance of our pain as it is so that self-interest is taken out of the equation when we choose to react to the injustice we see. Revenge is not helpful, acceptance is unstoppable. When we act from a place of acceptance and love, we include those on the margins of society and give them a voice in our ongoing human narrative. And everyone is better for it.

EDITORIAL REVIEW

The Moment of Lift raises our eyes to the blind spots of a fallen world. It's not the rant one expects from the feminist mantra on the cover, but a profound and guided discussion that is accessible to all levels. You'll read it in a day but feel it for a lifetime.

Melinda has seen and heard things most of us glance over briefly in a statistic or a news headline. She has become so entwined with the plight of women around the world that it is impossible to tell whether it is her courage or theirs that fuels such tenacity for change and equality.

Bewilderingly, her story is easy to digest. It's fascinating that someone who walks daily in the realm of the rich and famous makes it sound like she isn't even aware of the glamour or privilege with which she interacts each day. She balances it out by carrying the intense suffering she witnesses as a motivator to do more.

Her life is relatable in that she openly admits to doubt and denial. It took her years to fully commit to what had to be done, but she never stopped moving forward in her work through the foundation. She did what she felt she could do, and then, when she was ready, she did so much more.

The timeline is often jumpy, but the author has come to these thoughts over the years through a myriad of pivotal encounters and personal reflections. There wasn't a clear date when her life's work appeared out of thin air, and by her own admission, she is still learning and growing. A genuinely compassionate heart is evident here with grit that scoops others up in the wave.

Melinda's journey is as much an internal one as it is a world-shaking, history-making voice for women on a global scale; it is a jumble of pain, passion, and hope. She describes her hope for her own children, revealing her own chorus line.

"I want them to see that in the universal human desire to be happy, to develop our gifts, to contribute to others, to love and be loved—we're all the same. Nobody is any better than anybody else, and no one's happiness or human dignity matters more than anyone else's" (Gates, p. 119).

The narrative includes other people's stories, true to the underlying message of the book that all human lives are of equal value. It evokes more than an engaged fascination with the subject—it compels action.

Chapter eight ends with a gut-punch to the male-dominated religions so influential in the laws and traditions that have kept women suppressed and disempowered through the ages. It makes sense to address such a controversial issue, but it takes the whole narrative up a level and may leave a slightly bitter aftertaste.

Overall, the tone is down to earth—the voice of humble, kind humanitarian. Yet the powerful message carried in its bosom cannot be ignored. There is more to be done—injustice continues when people are left out in the cold.

BACKGROUND ON AUTHOR

Melinda Gates grew up in Dallas, Texas, and was drawn to the tech industry by a teacher at her all-girls high school. She graduated from Duke University with a bachelor's degree in Computer Science and later added an M.B.A. from Duke's Fuqua School.

Mother of Jenn, Rory, and Phoebe, she is married to the founder of Microsoft, Bill Gates. The tech giant is also where she happened to start her career in software, foregoing an offer from IBM to join the fledgling company. She met Bill later, never imagining she would end up marrying him.

Since co-founding the Bill and Melinda Gates Foundation, the couple has worked tirelessly to reach the poorest people of the world with life-changing support. Among a myriad of meaningful philanthropic ventures, Bill and Melinda have developed vaccines, promoted education, funded medical research, and created agricultural programs.

Melinda's journey with global health issues led to her public leadership as a women's rights activist, largely focused on the empowerment of women as a catalyst for ending extreme poverty.

Melinda created Pivotal Ventures, which invests in the business ideas of women from minority groups. She is also a public speaker and practicing Catholic.

Melinda and Bill live in Seattle, Washington.

Made in the USA
Coppell, TX
07 January 2020

14189413R00020